D0407849

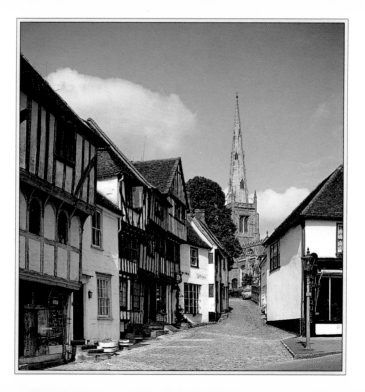

Tudor Britain

Tudor Britain

Photographs by Andy Williams
Text by Nicholas Best

WEIDENFELD AND NICOLSON
LONDON

Introduction

THE English emerged from a long dark tunnel at the end of the 15th century. From the murder of Richard II in 1400 to the death of Richard III in 1485, the country had been plunged into a series of fierce, bloody and ultimately fruitless civil wars, a seemingly endless struggle for power between the rival houses of York and Lancaster. First one house had seized the crown, then the other. First one king had been murdered in his bed, then another. It was not until 1485, when Richard III charged to his death on Bosworth field and the usurping Welshman Henry Tudor became Henry VII, that the Wars of the Roses came well and truly to an end. The new king promptly married Richard's niece, thus uniting the rival dynasties, and

set about creating, in the Tudors, one of the most successful of all England's royal families.

Henry was a shrewd man; he knew that prosperity was the key to a lasting peace. He immediately began to promote trade with Europe, while also imposing heavy fines on those barons who wanted to continue the war. He encouraged a rebirth of learning, financed the discovery of Newfoundland and carried on the building work of his predecessors, notably King's College Chapel at Cambridge, which had been abandoned during the fighting. His courtiers followed his example, taking advantage of the new stability to build lavish houses for themselves that were designed to show off their immense wealth, rather than protect them from attack. Others did the same - merchants, tradesmen, yeoman farmers - all sorts of people building houses designed to impress. So successful were they that much of what they built, under Henry and the later Tudors, has never been bettered. It was a golden age of British architecture.

FARMHOUSE

DATED 1593

*D*ATING from 1593, the year of Christopher Marlowe's murder at Deptford, this farmhouse is just one of the many hundreds that still survive from the period. Modern carpenters consider that their forebears used far more wood in the construction than they actually needed to.

HATFIELD HOUSE

HERTFORDSHIRE

*I*N 1558, Princess Elizabeth was sitting in the garden at Hatfield when she heard the news of Queen Mary's death and her own accession to the throne. The present house was almost entirely rebuilt by Robert Cecil, Earl of Salisbury, after Elizabeth herself had died.

Hall I' Th' Wood

Bolton

*W*ith a style all of its own, the timber-framed house dates from 1483, with a stone wing added in 1591. Samuel Crompton invented the cotton spinning-mule there, working secretly at night so that people thought the place was haunted.

LAVENHAM

SUFFOLK

*L*AVENHAM owed its prosperity in Tudor times to the wool and cloth trade. This row of houses, near the town centre, is typical of many.

BURGHLEY HOUSE

CAMBRIDGESHIRE

*M*AGNIFICENT by any standard, the house was built by William Cecil, Secretary of State to Elizabeth I. It still belongs to his descendants, now Marquesses of Exeter.

CANTERBURY CATHEDRAL

KENT

*O*N a site familiar to generations of Becket pilgrims, the main entrance to Canterbury Cathedral was completed in 1517. The statue overhead replaces one destroyed by the Roundheads, who used it for target practice.

———◆———

GREAT WALTHAM

ESSEX

$\mathcal{I}$N an age when most houses were still roofed with thatch, chimneys were an important consideration in Elizabethan architecture. These, in Essex, are typical of many throughout the country.

HAMPTON COURT

*C*ARDINAL Wolsey was flying too high when he built this magnificent palace for himself on the Thames. He was later forced to make a gift of it to Henry VIII, but that was not enough to save him from humiliation and disgrace.

SMALLHYTHE PLACE

KENT

*I*N the days when Smallhythe was a busy shipbuilding centre, this typical Kentish house was the official Port House. More recently, it was the home for many years of the actress Ellen Terry.

HARDWICK HALL

DERBYSHIRE

*R*EVOLUTIONARY for its time, the hall has as much glass as stone in its walls. It was built by the redoubtable Bess of Hardwick, who incorporated her initials (Elizabeth, Countess of Shrewsbury) on the top.

LOWER BROCKHAMPTON

WORCESTERSHIRE

*S*URROUNDED by its own moat, the manor house is a delight. It is approached through an archway in the gatehouse on the left.

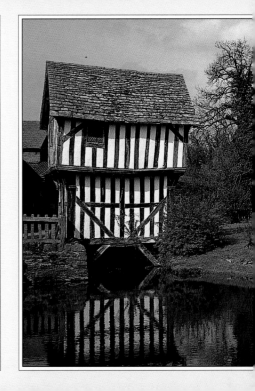

LITTLE MORETON HALL

*B*UILT by three generations of the Moreton family, this is one of the best examples of black-and-white architecture in the country. It has two secret rooms - one designed to be discovered easily, the other much harder to find.

———•◦•———

COMPTON WYNYATES

WARWICKSHIRE

*A*s was only sensible in troubled times, the main house is full of secret passages, sliding panels and concealed rooms. Henry VIII once stayed there, as did 400 parliamentary troops – without the owner's permission – during the Civil War.

KIRBY HALL

NORTHAMPTON

*E*VEN without a roof, Kirby is still one of the most beautiful Elizabethan houses in the country. It was begun by Sir Humphrey Stafford, but later passed to the Finch-Hattons, who still own the estate.

LORD LEYCESTER HOSPITAL

WARWICKSHIRE

*F*ORMERLY a guildhall, the building was turned into an almshouse for the old and disabled in 1571. Eight of Lord Leicester's 'brethren' continue to live there to this day.

LAMBETH PALACE

LONDON

*J*UST across the river from the Houses of Parliament, Lambeth has been the London home of the Archbishops of Canterbury for 700 years. The present buildings date from different periods, but the gatehouse, next to the parish church, is of mellow Tudor brick.

———•••••———

LONGLEAT

WILTSHIRE

*L*ONGLEAT shows Tudor architecture at its most impressive. Once a priory, it was massively redesigned by Sir John Thynne in the 1540s - one of the first large houses built entirely for show, and not for defence.

TRINITY COLLEGE CAMBRIDGE

CAMBRIDGE

*T*HIS is the gateway to Trinity, one of the most distinguished of all Cambridge's colleges. It was built by Henry VIII, whose statue stands above the entrance. Sir Isaac Newton's old rooms are next to the gateway on the right.

BURTON AGNES HALL

YORKSHIRE

*T*HE builder's daughter loved Burton Agnes so much that her dying wish was for her skull to remain there forever. It has been reburied several times, most recently in a wall of the great hall.

MAGDALEN COLLEGE OXFORD

OXFORD

*M*AGDALEN'S bell tower was completed in 1509. By tradition, the college's choral scholars sing a Latin hymn from the top, every Mayday morning at 5 a.m.

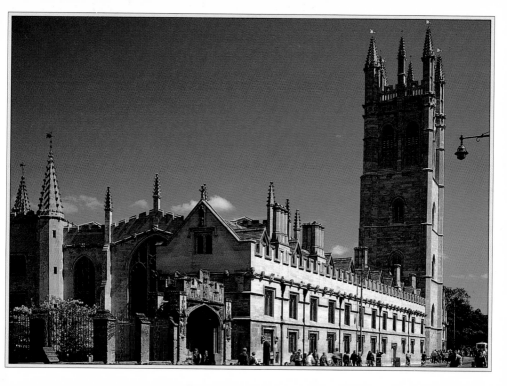

KNOLE
KENT

*O*NCE an archbishop's palace, Knole was greatly enlarged by Henry VIII. His daughter Elizabeth gave it to the Sackville-West family, who still live there. Virginia Woolf loved Knole so much that she used it as the model for her novel Orlando.

GREAT DIXTER

EAST SUSSEX

*F*AMED for its lovely garden, the house was almost in ruins at the beginning of this century. It was rescued by Edwin Lutyens, who restored the original building and added a 16th century extension – a derelict cottage, brought piece by piece from Benenden in Kent.

QUEENS' COLLEGE CAMBRIDGE

CAMBRIDGE

*T*HE President's lodge at Queens', dating from about 1540, is a particularly fine example of the timber and plaster architecture of the period. Erasmus may well have walked in the cloister below during his time at the college.

KENTWELL HALL

*B*UILT of mellow red brick, the hall is approached by a long avenue of lime trees, planted in the 1670s. Like so many Elizabethan houses, its ground plan takes the shape of an E, allegedly as a tribute to the monarch.

ACKNOWLEDGEMENTS

Text © Weidenfeld & Nicolson 1995
Photographs © Andy Williams

First published in Great Britain in 1995 by George Weidenfeld & Nicolson Ltd
Orion House, 5 Upper St Martin's Lane, London WC2H 9EA

All rights reserved. No part of this publication may be reproduced, stored in a retrieval
system, or transmitted in any form or by any means, electronic, mechanical, photocopying or
otherwise, without the prior permission in writing of the copyright owners.

British Library Cataloguing-in-Publication Data
A catalogue record for this book is available from the British Library

Cover and series design by Peter Bridgewater/Bridgewater Book Company
House Editor: Beth Vaughan

Front cover: The Guildhall, Lavenham, Suffolk
Half-title illustration: Thaxted, Essex
Frontispiece: Kings College, Cambridge
Introduction: Mary Arden's house, Warwickshire